T5-DHH-314

ILL ....
MILLS USE
....

Blackwater Regional Library
22511 Main Street
Courtland, Virginia 23837

Children's Authors

Christopher Paolini

Jill C. Wheeler

ABDO Publishing Company

visit us at
www.abdopublishing.com

Published by ABDO Publishing Company, 4940 Viking Drive, Edina, Minnesota 55435.
Copyright © 2007 by Abdo Consulting Group, Inc. International copyrights reserved in all countries. No part of this book may be reproduced in any form without written permission from the publisher. The Checkerboard Library™ is a trademark and logo of ABDO Publishing Company.

Printed in the United States.

Cover Photo: Random House
Interior Photos: Corbis pp. 6, 7, 8, 9, 13, 15, 16; © Don Maitz 1996, Lord of the Skies p. 11; Random House pp. 5, 17, 19, 23; © Stuart Conway p. 21

Series Coordinator: Megan Murphy
Editors: Heidi M. Dahmes, Megan Murphy
Art Direction: Neil Klinepier

Library of Congress Cataloging-in-Publication Data

Wheeler, Jill C., 1964-
    Christopher Paolini / Jill C. Wheeler.
        p. cm. -- (Children's authors)
    Includes index.
    ISBN-10 1-59679-765-7
    ISBN-13 978-1-59679-765-9
        1. Paolini, Christopher--Juvenile literature. 2. Fantasy fiction--Authorship--Juvenile literature. 3. Authors, American--21st century--Biography--Juvenile literature. I. Title. II. Series.

  PS3616.A55Z95 2006
  813'.6--dc22

                                                                2005023132

Contents

Writing Down Daydreams................................. 4

Family First 6

Homeschooling... 8

A Story Takes Root...................................... 10

Learning to Write Better 12

On the Road 14

Big Break... 16

Best Seller 18

The Trilogy Continues 20

Glossary 22

Web Sites 23

Index.. 24

Writing Down Daydreams

The story sounds like a fantasy. A 15-year-old boy from a rural Montana family writes a novel. The novel becomes a best seller. Suddenly, the boy and his family are millionaires! Well, this fantasy is reality for Christopher Paolini. Paolini is the author of the best-selling novel *Eragon*.

Eragon is the story of a young boy in a faraway kingdom. He finds a magic stone that hatches a dragon named Saphira. The boy, Eragon, and the dragon become best friends. Together, they set out to defeat an evil king.

Many parts of *Eragon* sound familiar. Even Paolini admits he borrowed a lot of ideas from other writers. Yet, Paolini never set out to write a best-selling novel. He says he was just a lonely boy looking for a way to entertain himself. He did that by writing down his own **vivid** daydreams.

Paolini says his family doesn't watch much television. But, he does play a lot of video games. Paolini claims to be unbeatable.

5

Family First

Christopher Paolini was born on November 17, 1983, in southern California. His father, Kenneth, had a background in photography. His mother, Talita, had trained as a **Montessori** teacher. Christopher also has a younger sister named Angela.

Kenneth and Talita believed family was very important. They made a special vow while on their honeymoon in Hawaii. They agreed their family would always come first. Even their jobs would center around their family.

Kenneth worked for a publishing company in Alaska for a while. Then the Paolini family settled in rural Montana.

Maria Montessori is the educator who invented the Montessori style of teaching.

Paradise Valley, Montana

They moved to a small house on the edge of the Yellowstone River. The house is in an area of mountains and forests called Paradise Valley.

Few job opportunities existed in Paradise Valley. But, the Paolinis made money as best they could. In 1997, Kenneth and Talita started a publishing business called Paolini International. The company published several books Kenneth and Talita wrote themselves. One was a book Talita wrote about education. It was based partly on her experiences teaching her own children.

Homeschooling

Christopher and Angela did not attend a traditional school. Instead, they were homeschooled. Homeschooling was one more way the Paolinis made their family come first. It also allowed Talita and Kenneth to offer their children the best education possible. They did not just want Christopher and Angela to learn facts. They wanted them to learn how to think.

Talita tried to make their lessons as fun as possible. For example, Christopher became interested in pirates. So, Talita made a special pirate map for him. She soaked the paper in tea and burned the edges to make it look like a real map.

Christopher began reading at an early age. He discovered fantasy books at age ten. He loved J.R.R. Tolkien's The Lord of the Rings

J.R.R. Tolkien

trilogy. His other favorites included *Beowulf* and *Jeremy Thatcher, Dragon Hatcher*. He estimates he has read more than 3,000 books!

Homeschooling also gave Christopher time to explore other interests. In addition to reading, he loves music, computer games, and movies. His family owns about 4,000 movies and watches one nearly every evening. Christopher also built his own **forge**, which he uses to make swords, knives, and **chain mail**.

Chain mail has many purposes. It was used as armor in medieval times. And today, scuba divers often wear chain-mail suits for protection when researching sharks.

A Story Takes Root

Christopher recalls spending many hours daydreaming about battling monsters and riding dragons. Sometimes it was all he had to do. Paradise Valley was a beautiful place. But, there was not a lot to do there.

Talita stopped homeschooling Christopher when he reached high school. Instead, he took a high school **correspondence course**. He graduated from that course when he was just 15 years old.

The Paolini family then had to make a decision. Now that Christopher had completed high school, he could go on to college. However, Kenneth and Talita decided Christopher was too young. So, he had to find something else to do for a while.

Christopher quickly came up with a way to fill his time. At age 14, he had started writing a story. It was a fantasy about a boy and a dragon. At first, he thought it would make a good movie. But later, he decided he wanted to write something that he would enjoy reading. And, he had plenty of time to focus on his story now that he was not in school.

In his story, Christopher used common elements from many fantasy novels, such as dragons and magic spells. But, he changed the ideas to make them his own.

Learning to Write Better

Paolini began reading about the elements of a good story. He studied ways to develop characters and plot. He learned how to turn a simple idea into a novel. And, he read about how to create strong characters and make his story flow smoothly.

Then, Paolini spent a month plotting his first book. He also outlined two **sequels**. He called the three books the Inheritance **Trilogy**. Each book in the trilogy features a new dragon.

Paolini spent the next 11 months writing the first book. The nearby Beartooth Mountains were the inspiration for the whole new world he created. He and his sister also made up three new languages. They turned to old **Norse** languages for ideas.

Near the end of 1999, Paolini finished the first **draft** of his story. He recalls it was easy to write. The story he had imagined for so long poured out of him. Then he read the first **draft** again and realized it needed work. So, he spent another year **revising** the **manuscript**.

Finally, Paolini showed the edited draft to his parents. They were amazed. The family agreed their publishing company should publish the manuscript. *Eragon* was born.

Paolini used the nearby Beartooth Mountains as the inspiration for the trilogy's setting, Alagaesia.

On the Road

Kenneth and Talita spent another year working with Christopher on the *Eragon* **manuscript**. They corrected **grammar** and moved some sentences. Paolini designed the artwork for the book's cover. He also drew a map of Alagaesia, the imaginary land where the story takes place.

Then, the Paolinis hired a local printer to produce a few thousand copies of the book in paperback. The printing took the last of the family's savings. In February 2002, *Eragon* was released.

Around the same time, Paolini received a full **scholarship** to Reed College in Portland, Oregon. However, he decided to help promote *Eragon* instead. The Paolini family contacted 135 schools and stores to arrange for visits. Many of the places had never had an author visit before.

Paolini wore a **medieval** costume during the readings and signings. Some days he spent eight hours in his costume, talking without a single break. If he was lucky, Paolini might sell 40 books at an event.

Over time, the book orders began to grow. Soon the Paolini house was filled with books ready to ship. *Eragon* was now the family's main source of money. Kenneth recalls that if the family did not sell books, they did not eat.

Paolini wore the clothing of a medieval storyteller during book signings for **Eragon.**

Big Break

The Paolini family spent a year on the road promoting *Eragon*. They traveled around the northwestern United States. Once they went as far south as Texas! They sold an amazing 10,000 copies of the book during that time.

Everything changed in summer 2003. Best-selling novelist Carl Hiaasen and his family were visiting Montana on a fishing trip. Hiaasen's stepson, Ryan, bought a copy of *Eragon* on

Carl Hiaasen is the author of Newbery Honor winner Hoot. Hiaasen has also written many adult books.

the trip. Once Ryan started reading it, he could not put the book down.

Hiaasen was curious, so he asked Ryan about the book. Ryan replied he liked it better than the Harry Potter books. Hiaasen quickly told his publisher about *Eragon*. The publisher was Alfred A. Knopf, which is a part of Random House. Soon, an editor at Knopf named Michelle Frey contacted the Paolinis. She asked them about purchasing the book.

Paolini designed the original cover image of **Eragon**. *The cover was changed to the above image when Knopf agreed to publish the book as the first part in the Inheritance Trilogy.*

The Paolini family knew they had a winning title on their hands. They hired a **literary agent** to represent them in their dealings with Knopf. Eventually, they agreed to let Knopf publish *Eragon*. They also sold the rights to the other two books in the Inheritance **Trilogy**. Suddenly, their money worries were history.

Best Seller

Frey trimmed the *Eragon* **manuscript** by about 20,000 words. And, Knopf created a new cover image for the 500-page book. It also printed 100,000 hardcover copies. *Eragon* was released on August 26, 2003. The book quickly jumped to the top of the best-sellers list for children's chapter books. At the time, *Eragon* even outsold some of the Harry Potter books!

Now, Paolini hit the road for Knopf. He traveled to many cities doing **media** tours. He even toured Great Britain in 2004 for the United Kingdom release.

As before, Paolini visited bookstores to promote the book and sign copies. He also visited with reporters and journalists. *People* and *Newsweek* carried stories about the young author. He was a guest on the *Today Show* and the *Late Show with David Letterman*, too. Luckily, he no longer had to wear his **medieval** costume.

After the book tours, Paolini returned to Montana. Now he had time to focus on the second book of the **trilogy**. It would be called *Eldest*.

Paolini wrote the first 60 pages of *Eragon* by hand. Fortunately, he learned how to type so he didn't have to handwrite the rest of the lengthy manuscript.

The Trilogy Continues

Eldest was released in August 2005. Paolini is now at work on the final book in the **trilogy**. He will not tell anyone but his sister the ending. However, he says the third book ends happily.

A movie **version** of *Eragon* is also in the works. Fox 2000 Pictures began working on the film in summer 2005. The movie is expected to be released in 2006.

Paolini's life has changed little since he became a successful writer. He still devotes most of his day to writing in his room on a computer. He spends his evenings watching movies with his family. He did take time out of his schedule to dig a hobbit hut in his backyard. The hut was complete with an eight-foot (2-m) hole underneath.

Paolini is not sure what he will do when he finishes the trilogy. He said he may take a vacation or he might catch up on his reading. Eventually, Paolini plans to write more books. That is good news for *Eragon* fans!

Family has always been important to Paolini. He even uses his family in his books. In Eragon, the character of the herbalist is based on Angela.

Glossary

chain mail - flexible armor made of interlinking metal rings.

correspondence course - a form of schooling in which lessons and exercises are mailed to the student. When completed, the lessons are returned to the school for grading.

draft - an early version or outline.

forge - a workshop or furnace where metal is heated and made into weapons, armor, or tools.

grammar - the system of rules that determines the correct way to speak, write, and use language.

literary agent - a person who represents an author.

manuscript - a book or article written by hand or typed before being published.

media - the medium of communication that includes television, radio, and newspapers.

medieval - of or belonging to the Middle Ages, which is a period of time from AD 500 to 1500.

Montessori - a method for educating children based on developing a child's ambition, senses and muscle training, and freedom through prepared lessons and games.

Norse - of or relating to Scandinavia or its languages, which include Norwegian, Swedish, and Danish.

revise - to change something in order to correct or improve it.

scholarship - a gift of money to help a student pay for instruction.

sequel - a book or movie continuing a story that began previously.

trilogy - a group of three books or movies that create a related series.

version - a different form or type from the original.

vivid - creating a strong or clear impression, especially relating to the imagination.

Web Sites

To learn more about Christopher Paolini, visit ABDO Publishing Company on the World Wide Web at **www.abdopublishing.com**. Web sites about Paolini are featured on our Book Links page. These links are routinely monitored and updated to provide the most current information available.

Index

A
Alagaesia 14
Alaska 6
Alfred A. Knopf 17, 18
B
Beartooth Mountains 12
Beowulf 9
C
California 6
E
education 8, 9, 10
Eldest 18, 20
Eragon (book) 4, 13, 14, 15, 16, 17, 18, 20
Eragon (movie) 20
F
family 4, 6, 7, 8, 9, 10, 12, 13, 14, 15, 16, 17, 20
Fox 2000 Pictures 20

Frey, Michelle 17, 18
H
Harry Potter books 17, 18
Hawaii 6
Hiaasen, Carl 16, 17
hobbies 8, 9, 10, 20
I
Inheritance Trilogy 12, 17, 18, 20
J
Jeremy Thatcher, Dragon Hatcher 9
L
Late Show with David Letterman 18
Lord of the Rings, The 8, 9

M
Montana 4, 6, 7, 10, 16, 18
Montessori 6, 7
N
Newsweek 18
O
Oregon 14
P
Paolini International 7, 13
People 18
R
Random House 17
Reed College 14
T
Texas 16
Today Show 18
Tolkien, J.R.R. 8
U
United Kingdom 18
Y
Yellowstone River 7

JAN 2 9 2007